Favorable Mutation:

The Rise of Unified Managed Accounts in Financial Services

Favorable Mutation:
The Rise of Unified Managed Accounts in Financial Services

Published by: Investmart
                 Brooklyn, NY 11205

ISBN: 1-450515-28-2
EAN13: 978-1-45051-528-3

Printed in the United States of America.

First Printing: January 2010

Favorable Mutation:

The Rise of Unified Managed Accounts in Financial Services

Jason G. Lampa, MBA

Investmart, Brooklyn, NY 11205

Table of Contents

Introduction

All Articles were first published on ProducersWeb

Remote viewing: The future of financial advice

As with any profession where high profits exist, fierce competition will ensue, leading to innovation and an exponential rise in the professional abilities of the individuals working within that industry. The wealth management industry is a perfect example.

It is certainly no secret that wealth management services are undergoing a paradigm shift with consequences that will affect the delivery of financial advice for the next 50 years and beyond. The ability to run a successful wealth management firm will depend on its members' ability to embrace change and to cater to the baby boomer generation while effectively marketing their services to their boomer client's children. The elite firms, the very best, will be staffed with consultants who are both Philomath's (seekers of knowledge) and polymaths (people in possession of great knowledge in many disciplines).

No, I am not a philosopher. However, I want to make certain that I do my part to prepare the financial advisor community for prosperity – now and in the future. Let us look at three ways that may help achieve this goal: reduce non-revenue generating activities, reach affluent investors around the globe and increase the amount of face-to-face interactions with clients and top prospects.

1

At the forefront of most successful firms is a systematic process to leverage technology and turn operational units into profit centers. Here are three ideas that can help your firm accomplish this in 2010, as well as ideas for a client appreciation event to celebrate your success with your new clients:

Voice recognition software (www.nuance.com) – If you see a keyboard in your office, throw it out the window. Keyboards cause carpel tunnel syndrome and are quite simply, inefficient. Dragon NaturallySpeaking Professional 9 enables financial services professionals to create documents and e-mails, fill out forms, and create proposals with just the sound of their voice. According to Nuance, Dragon NaturallySpeaking is about three times faster than typing, and up to 99 percent accurate.

The virtual world (www.secondlife.com) – The virtual landscape is the new frontier for many entrepreneurs. However, it is a powerful and fun way to engage clients, train employees and establish your brand as a 21st century polymath. The Second Life Grid is a 3D virtual world that empowers an organization to create a hub for communication and collaboration for both internal and external audiences.

Video conferencing (www.sightspeed.com) – SightSpeed Business, in my opinion, is the most effective solution for wealth management firms to efficiently add more clients, manage meetings with existing clients and communicate with internal audiences (i.e., centers of influence). Here is a partial list of some of the world-class services they offer:
  Multi-party video conferencing

- Web-based video communications
- Integrated video mail and chat

Remember, if wealth management firms are looking to differentiate their services from the competition, prospects and clients from soccer moms to corporate executives, are more comfortable and more willing to remain with a firm that makes its services convenient.

I sincerely believe the solutions and services these cutting-edge companies offer will help you differentiate your wealth management firm from the competitors. In closing, I would like to provide you with an idea to make your year-end client appreciation event something your clients will be speaking about for years.

Cloud 9 Living (www.cloud9living.com) – Cloud 9 Living was founded in Boulder, Colo. in 2005. According to their web site, their mission is to enhance people's lives through memorable experiences. Look at the following experiences they offer:

- Denver, Colo.: Urban Scavenger Hunt – Your clients will form into teams of six to eight players. You will then be given a list of 100 topics, questions and clues that are customized to meet the interests of your clients. What really makes this event stand out is that each participant will be given a CD of the pictures taken during the scavenger hunt. How many referrals do you think you could get from that alone?
- New York, NY: Murder Mystery Party – Based on the game Clue, your clients will be talking about this night for years. Your clients get to question suspects and solve the crime with the help of a comic detective. For this event, have five couples invite their closest friends or family members.
- In summary, we have talked about the competitive state of the wealth management industry, the ingredients of the most successful firms of the future and four ideas to make your firm stand out from others in your area. Let us get started!

Riding the baby boomer wave: Finding new ways to market your practice

As the baby boomer demographic begins to transition out of the accumulation phase, the conversations they share at cocktail parties have changed drastically. For investors who took part in the go-go days of the late 1990s, social gatherings became a platform for comparing the grandiose returns their financial advisors were generating in their portfolio. I am sure many of you experienced clients demanding to know why their portfolio only went up 45 percent, while the neighbors gloated over a 75 percent gain. It is amazing what a decade can do.

Now, instead of talks of astronomical returns, guests at the party are discussing concerns such as running out of money during retirement and finding an advisor they trust and who will educate them on topics like nursing home options for their parents. This new dialogue presents financial advisors with a tremendous opportunity to grow their practice, However, with the potential opportunity comes more participants entering the marketplace.

Throughout the financial services industry, you will find wealth management firms catering their message to the baby boomer generation. As these highly publicized demographic transitions into retirement, the challenge will be providing a comprehensive solution that will not only attract their attention, but also propel them into action. How does a wealth management firm accomplish this amidst the recent downturn in the global equity markets?

In this article, we will discuss the first two steps of the journey.

Identify the "hot" buttons for affluent baby boomers. The majority of the investors in this age demographic are concerned with three distinct financial outcomes:

- Caring for their aging parents and prudently managing assets coming from inheritance;

- Managing lump-sum distributions, such as IRA rollovers from substantial 401(k)/pension assets (Selling a business and strategic liquidation of stock options would also be included in lump-sum distributions);
- Overcoming longevity risk by following a retirement income strategy that will meet standard of living requirements for 30 plus years.

Be proactive in sourcing these potential clients to you by logging on to www.meetup.com.

Meetup claims to be the world's largest network of local groups. Having created a group of my own, I can tell you that this is an excellent way to get face-to-face interaction with thousands of potential clients in your local community.

Each Meetup group receives:

- A customized Web site;
- Message boards;
- Tools to prospect for members;
- Advice on how to maximize the success of the group.

For an example, visit: http://www.meetup.com/intimatenetworking.

Decide on the marketing activities that will be implemented to engage potential prospects. I suggest beginning this process by establishing three separate advisory boards. The purpose of these three groups is to exponentially grow your business. It is important to always remember this when choosing members for each group.

Step No. 1: Identify approximately eight to twelve of your top baby boomer clients who you think will take their role seriously and have the expertise to add value. Though you may know these individuals well, take the time to craft a plan that will lay out the structure for the board, as well as what will be required of them.

I recommend utilizing the following criteria to rank potential client-advisory members (point system 1–5; 1 = poor, 5 = outstanding):

- Personality
- Influence in community
- Net worth
- Business acumen

- Occupation

Step No. 2: Have your assistant contact your top 10 clients (excluding the ones in the first group) and schedule lunch appointments with each of them. During this lunch, ask them which business owners in the area they feel would be a good fit for your services. Judging by my experience, they will each most likely provide you with three or four names. As soon as you get back to the office, have your assistant schedule appointments for the following week with the business owners referred to you during your client lunch meetings. From this group, choose eight to 12 individuals (excluding accountants and lawyers). Be sure to place stringent requirements on qualifications. For example:

- Business must be in operation more than 10 years
- One or more of the major decision-makers is age 45+

Step No. 3: Utilizing the social networking tool LinkedIn, reach out to 10 accounting firms and 10 law firms, which reside in your area. Meet with each firm individually and decide on two accountants and two lawyers who will make up your third board of advisors.

Key benefits of forming an advisory board

- Keep your finger on the pulse of your practice .
- Increase face-to-face interaction with potential clients and existing clients.
- Build your brand as a super-networker within the community, which may lead to consulting opportunities and public speaking engagements.
- Learn about different industries and the universal ingredients of a profitable enterprise.
- Gather more assets from existing clients because of the increased perception of competence.

Create memorable events for the mature market

How many of you use event marketing as the core activity in your marketing strategy? This is a question I asked during a presentation I was giving to a group of advisors who were looking for ways to attract the 55+ market. Out of the 100 attendees, three raised their hands. I had each of them stand up and describe their experiences. All three were convinced that event marketing did not produce the results they expected.

"How much time did you spend planning the event?" I asked each of the three advisors who had hosted events in the past. The first two advisors were not sure. However, the third stated somewhere around two weeks of advance planning for the implementation of the event. This advisor had three wholesalers come in to speak about asset allocation and retirement income strategies to a crowd that included current clients and the one visitor they were instructed to bring.

The advisor and his staff, without an understanding of how a successful event is to be conducted, were bound to be disappointed with the results achieved from this event. For those advisors targeting the

55+ market, event marketing should be the core function of their marketing strategy. The foundation for exceptional events begins with taking the time to research your target audience.

Utilizing ethnography

Ethnography is a branch of anthropology wherein researchers evaluate people in their natural environment, rather than a formal research setting. This affords the opportunity to evaluate how people live their lives and what meaning a product or service has in their life.

In the March 2009 issue of the *Harvard Business Review*, Intel anthropologist Ken Anderson provides us with an understanding of why ethnographic research is so important to businesses and how the results affect the company's long-term strategy. At one point, Intel provided products only for businesses; however, in the mid-90s, executives got together and were curious to find out if residential consumers could become a distinct distribution channel.

Ethnographic research showed Anderson and his fellow anthropologists that marketing to users at home presented an enormous opportunity. So much so that Intel created a business unit that strictly focuses its effort on processors and platforms for home use.

According to Anderson, ethnography has proved so valuable at Intel that the company now employs two dozen anthropologists and other trained ethnographers, probably the biggest such corporate staff in the world. He also believes that ethnography is so beneficial that it will spread widely and help firms in every industry truly understand customers and adapt to fast-changing markets.

The good news for wealth management firms and individual financial advisors is that there have been many ethnographic studies already performed on the 55+ market. After all, they do control over

70 percent of the world's wealth. This research clearly shows us that people in this demographic:

- Enjoy sharing stories and experiencing new things.
- Are fiercely independent and want to provide input into each aspect of their life.
- Do not consider themselves to be a collective group, but unique individuals.
- Rely on peer-peer networks and utilize social media tools to find information on service providers they are thinking of using.

Based on this information, we can construct an event marketing campaign that will not only attract new prospects, but also keep people talking for months after the event.

Part 1: A creative idea for a memorable event
A popular hobby for the 55+ market is cooking. Evidence of this can be seen in the exploding popularity of the Food Network on cable TV. At foodnetwork.com, you can see that they position themselves as a unique lifestyle network that strives to cover way more than cooking.

"The network is committed to exploring new and different ways to approach food – through pop culture, competition, adventure and travel – while expanding its repertoire of technique-based information."

Their mission statement is speaking directly to the mature market, utilizing words such as "unique," "adventure" and "travel." A wealth management firm looking to attract more prospects may want to consider hiring a couple of chefs from the closest metropolitan city to teach a group of 10–15 prospects how to cook a certain style of food. After four weeks of training, hold a cooking competition for those prospects who participated in the training. Invite their friends and family as well as your current clients.

Part 2: Utilize social media tools to coordinate event

Anyone who has ever been responsible for planning even a small event understands how difficult they are to organize and execute. The people who need to be involved in order to make this a successful event need to be in constant communication. Columnist Ben Parr of Mashable.com provides some great tips on how this is done:

- **Skype:** Use Skype for conference calls and chats about event planning. Parr suggests utilizing Gchat and Tokbox to engage in audio and video brainstorming sessions.
- **Pbworks:** Parr recommends this wiki as the ideal tool for planning events. In his experience, Pbworks is an easy way to add notes, edit information and organize content. It is a favorite among organizers because of its business features, document-sharing features and RSS notifications.
- **Google Calender and Google Docs.** Parr likes these tools to assign tasks and meetings. For more detailed file collaboration and calendar system, Parr recommends Basecamp, a business project management solution.

Part 3: Sending invitations

Once you know who you want to invite, I suggest you set up a blog about the "Cook-Off" on Wordpresss, Squidoo or Typepad. Have someone on your administrative staff create the blog, and then post updates on a daily basis.

To invite prospects for the four-week training session, as well as friends/family and your current clients for the cooking competition, I recommend EventBrite.

Eventbrite is a provider of online event management and ticketing services. I have used Eventbrite for a couple of events and was very pleased with how easy it was to use. According to their Web site, their services will help users to do three basic tasks well:

1. **Publish.** Everything you need to create and easily personalize a custom Web page for your event.
2. **Promote.** The tools you need to spread the word about your event and maximize attendance.
3. **Sell.** The immediate power to sell tickets and collect money online.

Tip: Take the proceeds for the tickets sold to family and friends of the prospects, as well as your clients that attend the cooking competition, and donate them to a local charity chosen by the winner of the cooking competition.

Part 4: Promotion of event

To go along with the tools on Eventbrite, when I am responsible for promoting an event, I have found Twitter and Facebook to be effective platforms. I also recommend utilizing SlideShare, which will provide information about the cooking training and the competition in a professional PowerPoint presentation format.

With regards to the cooking competition, there may be people who want to see it, but can't attend for one reason or another. Consider setting up a live stream. Parr recommends Ustream and Mogulus for streaming the highlights of the event. Alternatively, if you choose to record the entire event, you can upload the video to YouTube.

Part 5: Make it memorable with post-event communication

To make sure this event leaves a lasting impression, keep it in the minds' eye of those that participated. On the Web site and blog that was initially established for the event, make sure there is a form that will capture contact information including e-mail and Twitter usernames. In addition, have your administrative staff send out personalized, hand-written thank you cards to each of the prospects and your clients who attended the competition.

Conclusion

As a financial advisor, you are probably looking at this and thinking that you would never have the time to pull it off. Event marketing is not easy, but once you get the first one out of the way, it will get easier.

Additional resources that you may want to consider when using social media:

- Evite
- Facebook
- Zvents
- Meebo
- Anyvite

In addition, here is one last tip: For firms that want to make event marketing a significant part of their client acquisition process, I recommend hiring a certified meeting professional.

Critical conversations: Baby boomers taking responsibility for aging parents

A failure to communicate can cause issues in every facet of life. More and more, the advisors I work with are saying that their baby boomers are having trouble starting conversations about financial, medical and end-of-life issues with their aging parents. This affords financial advisors a tremendous opportunity to cement their relationships with their baby boomer clients and, perhaps, garner the assets of the parents in the process.

I recently met with a financial advisor at a local restaurant in Brooklyn to provide her with some guidance on facilitating conversations between her baby boomer clients and their parents. The genesis of our meeting was the direct result of her acknowledgement of a growing need to provide answers to her client's questions about estate planning/legal considerations pertaining to their parents.

During our meeting, she shared with me that the biggest stumbling block her clients were facing was finding the courage to sit down with their parents and begin these critical conversations. I suggested that her clients initiate a dialogue with their parents by starting with questions similar to the following:

"We never know what tomorrow holds; and though I plan to be around for many years to come, I have begun to devise a plan in case something were to happen to me. Have you thought about doing the same?"

"Mom and Dad, you both know how much the beach house means to this family. We have gathered there every summer since I can remember. What would you like to have happen to the beach house upon your passing?"

"The other day a colleague shared with me that her father recently passed away after suffering a massive stroke. She went on to tell me that her father remained on life support for months because he never outlined what measures he would like to be taken to preserve his life. It created a hostile situation, as family members could not agree on what his wishes would have been. Have you thought about putting your wishes in writing to avoid such a problem for our family?"

During our meeting, I also provided her with a list of key points that I feel are important for financial advisors to remember in order to position themselves as a resource and advisor of choice.

Estate planning

A current will may be the most important document to a persons' estate. It provides direction on how they would like their assets distributed upon death. Many people pass on without a will, which leads to turmoil between surviving family members who are often unable to agree on what the deceased would have wanted.

A will should:

- Say how a person's property is to be distributed at death;
- Name the executor of the estate;
- Provide for the payment of cost incurred in settling the estate.

If the family does not have an estate attorney, a financial advisor can help to find one via their network.

Moreover, it is important that a will be treated as a living document. When dealing with aging parents, it is important to look for:

- Significant changes in financial circumstances;
- Change of residence to a new state or country;
- The birth of grandchildren.

Avoid probate

Probate is the court process of transferring property upon a person's death. It can be avoided by putting assets into a living trust, which may eliminate the need for probate. I will further discuss living trusts later in this article. The person does not have to give up control of their assets, and can be certain that their estates are settled quickly when they pass on.

Beneficiary options

Double-checking beneficiary designations can reveal how much a person's wishes may have changed throughout the years.

Life insurance, annuities, IRAs, brokerage accounts and other types of financial accounts may have a beneficiary designation. This designation names the person who will receive the proceeds at the time of the contract holders' death.

Nolan Baker and Mark Clair, known as The Retirement Guys, wrote about a real life scenario in their article, "Beneficiary mistakes cost a fortunate," (published on June 11 2009 in the *Toledo Free Press*):

Anne, before she got married and had children, named her sister as beneficiary on her retirement account. Later, she got married and had children, but the beneficiary designation was never changed. When Ann died in an unexpected accident, who got her retirement account? A Supreme Court ruling mandates that it go to the sister. The court stated that, although it was probably her intent to leave the money to her husband and children, the only evidence in writing stated it should go to her sister.

It is also important that a financial advisor show a basic understanding of the different legal options available. This will not only make them feel more confident when networking with attorneys, but will also empower their clients and their clients' aging parents to be comfortable when discussing estate planning issues with their attorney.

Power of attorney: A legal mechanism that empowers a designated person to make property, financial and medical decisions for the principal, the person who signs a power of attorney.

Medical power of attorney: This authorizes a designated person to make health care decisions for the parent in case they are not capable of making decisions for themselves.

Without this document, the decision will be put in the hands of the health care provider, which may not be what the parent would have wanted.

Advanced directive: This is a legal document written before someone is incapacitated by illness. It allows a person to state their preferences in regards to medical care. The two forms of advanced directives that are most widely known are a living will and a durable power of attorney for health care.

Living will: A living will instructs a hospital, physician or provider of medical care to administer no life-sustaining procedures if a person is terminally ill or permanently unconscious. For example: The parent has always said that if they were to slip into a coma, they would not want to be fed through a tube or have to be put on life support to keep their heart beating. The law requires that they say so in a living will.

Last will and testament: A last will and testament deals with financial and legal issues, contrary to a living will, which deals strictly with health care issues. This legal mechanism protects assets and helps minimize the chances of a person's estate being contested. Without this document, this person's estate will not be distributed based on their original wishes.

Advisors can increase their credibility even further by educating both adult children and their aging parents on basic types of trusts related to estate planning. Trusts may be effective tools to assist and make life easier for the surviving family members.

Types of trusts

Irrevocable living trusts – When an irrevocable living trust is established, the creator gives up control of the assets to the trustee. This means the creator of the trust no longer has the legal right to control the assets in the future, unless the creator is also the trustee.

Revocable living trusts – For those who want to maintain control of their assets, a revocable living trust can place property in a trust, while still giving the creator the legal right to take the assets back by revoking the trust.

Reasons to use irrevocable trusts:

- Reducing estate taxes: Irrevocable life insurance trusts (ILITs) are commonly used to remove an asset from a person's estate. The person who transfers assets into an ILIT is handing those assets over to the trustee and the designated beneficiaries of the trust so that the person no longer has ownership of the assets. Since the person no longer owns the assets, they cannot be taxed when the person later passes away.
- Asset protection: Another use of irrevocable trusts is to provide asset protection for the person who makes the trust and their family. The assets are placed into an irrevocable trust, the person who made the trust is giving up complete control of the assets, and therefore, the trust assets cannot be reached by a creditor of the person who created the trust. Family members can be the beneficiaries of the irrevocable trust, thereby providing the family with the assets, but outside of the reach of creditors.
- Charitable estate planning: A popular use of an irrevocable trust is charitable estate planning via a charitable lead trust or charitable remainder trust. The person creating the trust distributes

assets into a charitable trust while they are living; in turn receiving a charitable income tax reduction in the year the transfer was made.

Reasons to use revocable living trusts:

- Assets held in the name of a revocable living trust at the time a person becomes mentally incapacitated can be managed by their disability trustee instead of by a court-supervised guardian or conservator.
- As mentioned earlier, assets held in a revocable living trust at the time of a person's death will pass directly to the beneficiaries named in the trust agreement and avoid probate.
- By avoiding probate with a revocable living trust, the person's trust agreement will not be included in a public record for all to see. This will keep the details about the assets and who received them private.

Note: A last will and testament that has been admitted to probate becomes a public record that anyone can read.

Additional Resources for those caring for aging parents:

Elder Life Planning – www.elderlifeplanning.com
The National Academy of Elder Law Attorneys (www.naela.org)

Jason G. Lampa

Retirement arbitrage:
Boomers head south to enjoy retirement

Most U.S. baby boomers are not prepared for their retirement. During the past 18 months, they have seen their retirement accounts and homes – which they were counting on to fund their retirement years – lose significant value. In addition, rising health care costs and college tuition are eating away at their current income and have caused American boomers to look for alterative options for retirement.

The generation responsible for adventure travel is now looking to spend their retirement years abroad. The number of Americans older than 65 years old is expected to double by 2030, according to the U.S. Census Bureau, and many of those Americans will reside outside the U.S. Financial advisors need to be aware of this trend and how it may affect their businesses going forward. It is possible that those clients will tap into their resources for solutions on retiring abroad, and as their advisor, it will help build your credibility if you can assist them in their effort.

Central America and Mexico are becoming the most popular destinations for American retirees. For example, the number of U.S. senior citizens living in Panama doubled between 1990 and 2000, according to a Panama Census.

Benefits to retiring overseas

- Lower cost of living
- Tax deferrals
- Tax exemptions
- Senior citizen discounts

Central America and Mexico are a short distance from the U.S. by plane, allowing boomers to make the transition to living abroad without losing touch with friends and family. The areas also offer

19

beautiful weather, miles of beaches and friendly people. Individual countries gaining popularity with American baby boomers include:

- Brazil
- Panama
- Nicaragua
- Mexico
- Costa Rica

Brazil

A strong economy, affordable housing and a highly developed infrastructure make Brazil an ideal place for boomers in retirement. Whether in the Hamptons, Florida or Mexico, beachfront property usually is a valuable investment. Brazil falls into this category, as well. Boomers may be shocked and excited to know that a house on the water in Brazil is approximately 1/10 to 1/20 the price of buying a beach house in Ft. Lauderdale. To go along with affordable property, Americans retiring in Brazil will be happy to know that the lower standard of living will allow them to hire live-in cleaning staff. Examples of staff include:

- Gourmet chefs
- Cleaning staff
- Groundskeeper
- Chauffeur
- Event planner

In total, the full staff listed above costs between $1000–2000 per month (depending on a number of factors).

Another consideration is safety. In Brazil, the major crime centers are located in poor sections of Rio de Janeiro and Sao Paolo. Within the past couple of years, the Brazilian government has made civilian safety a key initiative as they look to secure the 2016 Olympics.

Panama

Known for years for its volatile political environment, Panama is now a safe retirement haven for American boomers with a cost-of-living equivalent to that of the United States in the 1960s. Looking to attract foreign retirees, Panama has one of the most generous incentive programs in the world. Typical discounts include:

- Fifty percent off of movies and sporting events;
- Fifty percent off of hotels Monday through Thursday;
- Twenty-five percent to 30 percent off of transportation;
- Twenty-five percent off at restaurants;
- Property tax remains frozen until a person sells their home. This would mean that your taxes would not go up as the area develops. Moreover, on new homes, you can get a 20-year deferral from taxes.

Panama offers excellent medical benefits and state-of-the-art hospital facilities in its major cities. Many of the doctors in Panama are trained in the U.S., and the standards at the top facilities are equivalent to those seen in hospitals in the U.S. According to InternationalLiving.com, prices for prescription drugs are low as well, because manufacturers price them for the market. Moreover, many drugs that require a prescription in the States are available over-the-counter in Panama.

Costa Rica

Despite having one of the highest standards of living in Latin America, purchasing power is greater in Costa Rica than it is in the United States and Canada. According to EscapeArtist.com, most areas offer housing costs less than those seen in the U.S., and hired help, as in

Brazil, is incredibly inexpensive. A recent study by the *Miami Herald* rated Costa Rica the 27th safest country for investment of 140 countries surveyed. That may not seem all that impressive, until you consider the U.S. was ranked No. 22. In addition, *Fortune* magazine ranked San Jose Latin America's fifth best city to do business in, and placed it within the 25 best cities in the world. According to the report, *Fortune* considered the city's ability to create opportunity for its residents, its business climate and how well it can satisfy the business needs of companies that invest there.

Costa Rica has had a stable democracy since 1949. According to babyboomer-magazine.com, it has not been subject to the kind of political civil unrest that has tragically set back progress in neighboring countries, nor was its progress impeded by these nearby conflicts.

The bottom line is that American baby boomers are finding that there are options outside the United States where they can enjoy their retirement years. The generation that changed everything is now utilizing their creativity to change the way we view retirement. As mentioned earlier, with the rising costs and diminishing values in both their retirement accounts and homes, be on the lookout for more American retirees heading south to live the retirement of their dreams.

Through adversity comes innovation

In the long history of humankind, those who learned to collaborate and improvise most effectively have prevailed" – Charles Darwin

An international genetics project called The Genographic Project recently discovered that modern humans almost became extinct approximately 70,000 years ago. In fact, before humans left the continent of Africa, the number of human beings existing on earth was under 2,000. Fortunately, for us, our ancestors escaped extinction by the skin of their teeth, providing an important lesson in the power of adversity and how it spurs innovation.

Based on mitochondrial DNA testing, scientists postulate that modern humans arrived on earth 200,000 years ago. The need for innovation was not necessary until about 130,000 years ago, when the climate on earth changed. No longer the beneficiaries of a warm tropical climate, our ancestors experienced a massive drought lasting approximately 60,000 years. Isolated from each other and living in tiny groups, there were two choices: extinction or innovation.

The almost inhabitable conditions forced humans to create new methods of hunting, better hunting tools and to develop their speech communication skills. Eventually, the climate improved, and armed with better skills, the human race flourished.

Much as our ancestors narrowly avoided extinction, so too, the global financial services industry narrowly survived a catastrophic collapse in 2008. The competitive landscape has significantly changed, creating both challenges and amazing opportunities. Those challenges include:

- Prospects are harder to find;
- Profit margins are falling;
- Clients expect more services for less cost;

- Investors want investment products that mitigate risk and provide consistent income;
- Social innovation and technological innovation is driving growth.

The wealth management firms that will survive and thrive, both now and in the future, focus their attention on three things:

- Human capital
- Innovation
- Profitability

Becoming an elite firm does not happen overnight. Before the transformation process to HIP is fully implemented, a well-organized operational structure and firm-wide evaluation must be completed.

Stage 1: Talent level and outsourcing

Evaluating the efficiency of your operational structure begins with assessing the current talent level of employees. In most average organizations, the distribution of talent is concentrated in a select few, who carry the burden of the underperformers. It is often hard for decision-makers at smaller firms to distant themselves emotionally from their staff, which inhibits them from making good business decisions. I recommend evaluating employees based the following criteria:

1. Work Ethic – 30 percent
2. Creativity – 30 percent
3. Team-Oriented – 30 percent
4. Investment Knowledge – 5 percent
5. Sales Skills – 5 percent

Work ethic, creativity and the ability to be a productive member within a team environment, in my opinion, should make up 90 percent of the evaluation process. Almost anyone of average intelligence can learn the fundamental concepts of financial markets. Most people of average intelligence can learn how to sell a concept, service or product. The difference between top performers and low-end performers comes down to traits that are very hard to learn or take a significant amount of time to learn, time which small financial services firms do not have.

You many notice that I do not include operational-based skills as part of the criteria. Most, if not all, operational activities can be outsourced. These include:

1. Asset allocation and fund management
2. Compliance
3. Marketing and branding
4. Technology systems and software
5. Accounting and account aggregation
6. Practice management
7. Education and training

Making the decision to make the transition from investment managers to asset gatherers is not as drastic as some may believe. I would even go as far as saying that firms can increase their perception as wealth managers by moving to this model. When a wealth management firm is managing the investments in-house, it is extremely difficult to get the perspective necessary to make objective decisions. It's human nature to look for evidence to support our decisions. Except for a small group of wealth management firms that have an in-house investment staff (8–10 people), most firms are not going to take the time to look for evidence that goes against their investment outlook or strategy. Looking at the opposite side of the coin is the reason why firms should look to utilize turnkey asset management platforms to manage their clients' money. These firms are in the business of managing managers and have the resources to include tax-harvesting, risk management and inserting the right investment vehicle for specific asset classes.

The decision to outsource services for increased operational efficiency does not mean that the operations staff gets put on waivers. The hope is that these employees can move into roles that generate revenue for the firm.

The process of evaluating current employees, recruiting to fill gaps and outsourcing operation tasks should take between three and six months.

Stage 2: How are we perceived?

If you have been in the financial services industry long enough, you know the importance of developing a brand. Until recently, many of the firms that I have worked with considered building their brand as a secondary marketing function. More than that, most firms do not have a strategic plan to create their brand. Going forward, I argue that developing distinguishable brand in target markets is necessary for survival.

It is important to remember that people often lack the knowledge to make informed decisions, especially when it comes to hiring a financial advisor. They are constantly bombarded with advertisements and sales pitches. In the restroom, in a taxi, at the grocery store; no matter where you go, there are video streams. This forces potential clients to make decisions on a subjective basis, which is why creating a memorable brand is so important.

The first step in the process is gathering feedback from your existing clients. Have an employee go to surveymonkey.com and create a 10 question survey that focuses on the reasons they chose you.

After you receive their feedback, have your team meet with your board of advisors, which should consist of small business owners in the area and your top wholesalers.

Take three to four hours to integrate three sets of opinions:

1. Feedback from your clients
2. Feedback from your board
3. The viewpoint of you and your team

There are five questions that the above should answer, which will provide you a clear brand message:

1. What are the top three reasons clients hire us?
2. How do we make a difference in client's lives?
3. Why are we in this business?
4. What can clients expect when working with us?
5. What makes us different?

Retirement Plans Available for Small Business Owners

The obvious question is 'Why should you, as a small business own-er, set up a retirement plan for you and your employees?' Actually, the benefits are many and it is a 'win-win' situation for you, your business and your employees.

As an individual, retirement can last for 30 years or more. Stud-ies have shown that a retiree will need up to 80% of his/her annual income to retire comfortably. Also, the average monthly payment from Social Security Administration as a retirement benefit is only $1,153 – and that is not a lot to enable comfortable retirement living. Therefore, some form of retirement plan outside of the government Social Security plan is necessary.

Setting up a small business retirement plan allows for investing now to gain financial security for when you and your employees retire in the future. In addition, both you and your employees get significant tax advantages, plus other incentives.

As a business benefit, employer contributions are tax deductible and assets in the plan grow tax-free, with compounding interest. Your business may also be eligible for certain tax breaks, tax credits and other incentives for starting a retirement plan. As well, busi-nesses who offer retirement plans tend to attract and retain better employees. Along with that goes the savings involved in hiring and training new employees.

For employees there are also benefits, aside from the obvious one that they will have a better retirement in terms of financial security. The employee benefits because the tax on employee con-tributions and investment gains in the plan are deferred until the monies are distributed. Contributions can be made through payroll deductions so the employee does not even miss the money being contributed into the plan. Typically, there are also flexible plan op-tions available.

Now that you know that setting up a small business retirement plan is beneficial for you, your business and your employees, let us look at some of the types of plans available.

Single (k)

Especially with a small business, a Single (k) retirement plan is a flexible, easy and cost-efficient way to maximize retirement savings. This type of plan is for businesses that are operated and run by a single owner who also may have part-time employees. Typically, it is for sole proprietorships, closely-held family businesses and corporations.

A Single (k) retirement plan offers the benefits of a 401(k) plan with the flexibility offered in profit sharing plans. With this type of plan, annual contributions of both salary deferral and profit-sharing contributions are allowed. Taxes are deferred until distribution. As a bit of further information, the Single (k) plan is not protected against creditors and/or lawsuits unless the plan covers at least one other employee besides the owner.

Single Defined Benefit Plan

The Single Defined Benefit plan is for those single employers (as opposed to the multi-employer defined benefit plan) wishing to set up a retirement plan. Any business owner or self-employed individual is eligible for this type of plan as well as employees who have worked at least 1,000 hours during the past year (or 2 years if there is no vesting period). There are no set limits to the contributions, but the contributions are based on actuarial assumption. The maximum retirement payout is $185,000 or 100% of the average of the 3 highest consecutive earning years. The vesting period is determined by the employer and employees cannot contribute to the plan.

This type of plan works best for older employers who are looking to save a lot of retirement monies over a short period. This type of plan also may be expensive and not very flexible because contributions are not optional and the actuary determines the contribution/ deduction limit.

Simplified Employee Pension Plan (SEP)

The SEP is a simplified plan that allows employers to contribute toward their own retirement and for their employees. The administrative costs for setting up a SEP plan are typically lower than plans that are more complex. In this type of plan, employers contribute to a conventional IRA (Individual Retirement Account) for themselves and each of their employees, subject to certain restrictions.

SEPs can be set up with businesses of any size, even if you are self-employed. The employer must adopt the SEP plan document and typically cannot have any other retirement plan in place. The financial institution that holds the SEP can have several investment funds for employees to choose. There are no filing requirements for this plan because the financial institution that holds the SEP-IRA's handles most of the paperwork.

The SEP plan also may have a flexible contribution obligation, which makes it a good plan if cash flow may be an issue. For example, contributions for employees may be larger in good cash flow times or contributions may be reduced when business is down – but the contribution rate must be the same for all employees. With this type of plan, only employer contributions are accepted. Employees cannot contribute to the plan.

Individual Retirement Account – IRA

Although it is often thought that IRAs are generally for individuals, employers can also set up and fund IRAs for their employees. An employer can set up a Traditional IRA (or a Roth IRA) with a payroll deduction plan. The employee authorizes a set amount to be deducted from their pay, with the remainder of the pay going back to them. At retirement, what the employee receives depends on the funding of the IRA and what the earnings or income is on those funds.

A Traditional IRA offers tax advantages to the employee, in that the earnings may not be taxed until the funds are distributed. A Roth IRA operates a little differently from a Traditional IRA in that the contributions to a Roth IRA are not tax deductible whereas they may be in a Traditional IRA. In addition, the distributions and earnings are not included as income in a Roth IRA. For both, however, earnings remaining in the account are not taxed. It is only distribution of funds that affects the taxing.

Both types of IRAs can be set up as a payroll deduction plan, and are available at different financial institutions, banks, insurance companies and brokerage firms.

Simple IRA

The Simple IRA plan gives small business owners a simplified method of making contributions towards their own and their employee's retirement funds. It is a savings incentive match where the employees can choose to make salary reduction contributions towards their retirement savings and the employer matches the amount of the contribution. The employer can match the contribution amount dollar-for-dollar or can make a percent contribution as a non-elective contribution. That means the employee does not necessarily have to contribute anything towards their IRA, but they will still receive the employer contribution into their IRA.

The basic rules for a Simple IRA plan are as follows: This plan is available for small business owners with 100 employees or less, who do not have any other retirement plans. The employer must match dollar-for-dollar up to 3% of the employee's salary (some years may be as low as 1%) or the employer must contribute an amount equal of up to 2% of the employee's salary (to a maximum of $4,600) whether or not the employee makes any contributions to the plan.

Vesting (the time when the employer contribution is owned fully by the employee) for this plan is immediate. The contributions are all made directly into an IRA that is set up for each individual. The employee typically has several investment choices and investment options, according to the financial institution the employer has partnered with.

Profit Sharing Plans

Any business owner or self-employed individual is eligible for a Profit Sharing plan, and employees who have worked at least 1,000 hours during the past year (or 2 years if there is no vesting period) are also eligible. Profit sharing plans allow the business owner or employee a chance to share in the company's profits. The amount of the annual contribution will vary from year to year, based on the company's performance and is determined by the plan's benefit formula set up by the employer. The vesting period is also determined by the employer. Employees may be allowed to take out loans with this type of plan and it has greater design flexibility. However, because minimum coverage tests must be met, it can exclude some employees. (The minimum coverage rule for the 401(k) requires that employers make the plan available to a cross-section of employees and must satisfy the ratio-percentage test or the average benefits test.)

Since this type of plan is usually more complex to set up and operate, administration of a Profit Sharing plan is typically handled by a professional.

Therefore, as a small business owner, you now have a number of options to set up a retirement plan that would suit you, your business and your employee's needs. Setting up a retirement plan is an excellent way to allow your small business to offer the best opportunities for retirement savings – and with the tax advantages, incentives and other benefits, setting up a retirement plan for you and your employees just makes good business sense.

10 ways financial advisors can attract baby boomers in 2010

Between the years 1946 and 1964, it is estimated that 76 million babies were born in America. Known as the baby boomers, they are now reaching their retirement years in a drastically changing economy.

Baby boomers are in a transition phase, where their focus is shifting from asset accumulation during their "earning" years to income generation for their upcoming retirement phase. Studies reveal that previously, many investors were overly optimistic about their retirement visions. Where once boomers thought that their pension plans would suffice to get them through their retirement years, this is now becoming an issue, especially with the changing economy. Assets invested in defined contribution plans, individual retirement accounts (IRAs) and non-qualified accounts will develop into the major source of income for these future retirees. Nevertheless, boomers now have to contend with the fact that the pensions they were relying on may not exist for them in the future.

The inherent challenges they now must face include:

- Decreasing Social Security benefits
- Growing need for account-type pension plans
- Reduced pension plans in the face of the current global economy
- Rising health care costs, made even more of an issue due to the aging population
- Increased life expectancies due to better diet, health care and medical advancements

With the changing economy and the new challenges being faced, a more realistic approach needs to be considered. Financial advisors need to readjust their thinking to find ways to attract boomers in 2010.

They need to be aware of the recent economic crisis and find solutions for retirees that will be sustainable across the variable market environments. Boomers have essentially run out of time to recoup the losses they have suffered from the recent economic crisis.

Of course, the chief responsibility of financial advisors will be to educate boomers in a new way of thinking about their finances. Financial advisors need to shift the focus of upcoming retirees into thinking more about retirement planning strategies and restructuring their portfolios to better suit their retirement needs. They will need to honestly assess the clients' vision of retirement and develop realistic and sustainable retirement savings models. They need to be prepared to come up with ways that provide a reliable income source once an individual stops working.

Past retirement savings included 401(k)s and IRAs, which have suffered the worst consequences of unfavorable market changes. Financial advisors need to shift to investment strategies where boomers take greater individual responsibility for their retirement plans, rather than relying on government funding. They need to focus on generating a sustainable retirement income stream from accumulated pension assets.

Here are 10 ideas for financial advisors to attract baby boomer business in 2010:

1. Investment products that address the decrease in accumulation of funds and focus more on retirement-specific needs such as rising health care costs and inflation should be presented. Offering products that provide protection against inflation is a sensible way to attract boomer business.
2. More emphasis should be placed on product choice and financial advice in the future. In the changing economic climate, the general product range should take into consideration the increased volatility, instability and uncertainty of capital markets.

3. Financial advisors should have a plan to put a fund-withdrawal system in place consistent with retirement spending. Life expectancy should be taken into account so that the money does not run out and the plan is not outlived.

4. Financial advisors should offer products that have the flexibility to cover unanticipated expenses. Unexpected expenses could include a new roof for the house, a car repair or even unexpected medical bills, all of which may require funding not supplied within the regular fund-withdrawal system.

5. Another idea is to offer a product that has the option to leave an inheritance. People are always interested in what they can leave behind for the betterment of their children or grandchildren.

6. Financial advisors should advise greater diversification in the products they offer to spread the risk of investment. Boomers have less time to recover from any losses suffered, so diversification helps to cover longevity risks in a variable market.

7. Within the baby boomer community, two housing trends are emerging. The first is with respect to downsizing. Discussing downsizing is another business strategy idea. Within this area of boomer households, children have grown and moved on to their own pursuits, leaving the parents alone in a house that may be too big for them. Even with the current decline in housing price trends, downsizing to a smaller more manageable house would not only reduce monthly housing expenses, but could also lead to acquired home equity that could potentially be invested for retirement purposes.

8. Although many boomers are downsizing their living arrangements, the second trend reveals some are actually upgrading to bigger, more expensive houses. The more financially secure are finding homes situated along waterfronts, ski resorts and in areas that are more desirable. This leads to a different invest-

ment strategy that financial advisors can take advantage of. The wealth of these retirees needs to be readjusted to accommodate their new living arrangements.

9. Many boomers are leaning towards a continuing work platform in their later years. In fact, it is estimated that 75 percent of all boomers intend to keep working throughout their retirement. Although they may be retiring from current jobs, many are considering new careers or businesses geared towards their present interests to keep them occupied in their retirement years. Taking into account, this new source of income, along with their retirement savings plan, creates another source of discussion and possible investment business.

10. In recent studies, it was found that an astonishing 50 percent of all baby boomers were still raising one or more young children and/or providing support to their elderly parents. With this in mind, financial advisors should amend retirement investment plans to include support for these other family members.

Baby boomers present a great opportunity for financial advisors to create new business. It is a vast market that really needs the help of a financial professional. With the downside in the economy, boomer retirement needs in 2010 are drastically different from retirees in previous times. Financial advisors need to re-adjust thinking patterns and investment strategies to attract this new phase of boomer business.

Investment Opportunities in India for the Mass Affluent

The mass affluent, as defined as those individuals with financial assets of at least $110,649 U.S, view the on-going financial crisis as an investment opportunity over the mid to long-term. At the present, they are gathering information to make informed investment decisions. Investments in emerging markets are high on their list of opportunities and more than 50% of the mass affluent have shown an interest in India.

With India being the second most populous country and the largest democracy in the world, it is no wonder that it has the potential for enormous growth in investment opportunities. India offers one of the largest economies in the world and is the fourth largest economy in terms of purchasing power.

One of the main reasons for the interest in Indian investments is because of the country's growth potential in the IT sector. There is also an expectation for expansion in domestic demand. To go along with this, India has a well developed knowledge industry and is progressing in the research and development (R&D) infrastructure and technical and marketing services.

There are many other reasons that the mass affluent are considering India as a golden opportunity for investment. India is in a strategic location with access to the vast domestic and South Asian markets. The rapidly growing consumer market consisting of upwards of 300 million people suggests a fantastic market for consumer goods, which is estimated to grow at a rate of 8% per year. India also offers one of the largest manufacturing bases in the world in all manner of manufacturing sectors. They also have one of the largest pools of scientists, engineers, technicians, accountants, lawyers and mangers present in the world today (available at competitive costs), and they have a rich base of mineral and agricultural resources.

India is one of the places where foreign investment is welcome. They are seeking foreign investment. Approval is required for some foreign investments, but is automatic in over sixty categories of industries. Their financial sector is sophisticated with a vibrant capital market consisting of 22 stock exchanges with over 9,000 companies listed and market capitalization of $154 million (U.S.) (March,

1996). Their policy environment provides freedom of entry, investment location, and choice of technology, production, import and export. They also offer a well-balanced package of fiscal incentives.

Another great appeal for the mass affluent investing in India is that it offers ease of interaction between India and the States. Although the country has 17 official languages, English is widely spoken and understood, and most workers are well educated. Foreign brand names are also freely used.

To sum up some of the more popular investment opportunities in the Indian market, herewith are a couple of industry reviews:

INVESTMENT INDUSTRY: One of the most discussed areas of investments in India has been in Foreign Direct Investment (FDI). This is an investment defined as "investment made to acquire lasting interest in enterprises operating outside of the economy of the investor". The foreign investor and the FDI form a relationship, which together forms a Trans-national Corporation (TNC). With India being rated among the top emerging nations and their current liberalization policies, rich dividends are being paid to the economy as a whole, in which the foreign investor can take part.

SOFTWARE INDUSTRY: The IT sector in India is rapidly growing, with most countries of the world relying on Indian software companies and firms for software development activities. India possesses the reputation of global competency in the IT field. More and more IT companies in India are receiving the ISO 9000 certification, and it is believed that India will soon have the highest number of ISO 9000 certifications in the world. At present, the Indian software industry is estimated to be worth $1.2 billion (U.S.). The downside to this area, though, is that there is a vast out-flow of IT professionals to other countries. It is believed, however, that this can be overcome by a more stable political economy.

BANKING INDUSTRY: There are two categories of banks in India—scheduled banks and non-scheduled banks. Scheduled banks are comprised of commercial banks and co-operative banks, of which there are approximately 67,000 branches across India. With financial reforms within the industry, 14 major banks were nationalized in 1969. This lead to a shift from Class banking to Mass banking and the growth of the banking industry since that time has been a continuous process.

The present banking scenario in India is thought to be in a transition phase. Public Sector Banks accounting for more than 78% of the total banking industry assets are burdened with too many non-performing assets, large labor issues and a lack of modern technology.

Private Sector banks, though, are more promising. They lead in internet banking, mobile banking and phone banking. They still, however, have a labor issue.

Foreign banks in India are still considered likely to succeed.

METAL INDUSTRY: The aluminum and metal industries form one of the strongest industries in the Indian economy. India possesses large deposits of natural resources, in the form of minerals such as copper, chromite, iron ore, manganese, bauxite, and gold. (The India aluminum industry falls under the non-iron based category, which includes the production of copper, tin, brass, lead, zinc, aluminum and manganese.)

The Indian metal industries sector has experienced substantial success in the previous decade. It is fast developing and the advancement of technologies is creating even faster growth, with international and domestic resources being significant in the rapid development of this field. Investment in this industry has a potentially bright future. In fact, it is believed that the Indian aluminum industry has the potential to become one of the largest players in the global aluminum market.

Although all of the above paints a wonderful picture of investing in India with the possibilities being almost limitless for overseas business and the market potential great, there are still some difficulties and challenges to be overcome. Because of its past semi-socialist self-sufficient economy and its previous distrust of foreign business, many companies still see India as a difficult market, and slow to change. Foreign investors should take India 'as it is' and develop a good understanding of the Indian market before taking the plunge into investments.

There is no doubt that India's past political changes have been a large part of India's investment opportunities in the past. There have been two major regime changes in the last decade, but the transfer of power has been democratic and peaceful which goes a long way to reassure potential investors of the changing direction that India sees for its future.

UNIFIED MANAGED ACCOUNTS

Chapter 1
The Movement from SMAs
to UMAs

Over the past several decades, the account structure and asset management options available to investors have shifted from the most basic of accounts, a brokerage account, to the managed accounts of today. Historically, affluent clients have preferred fee-based advisory services that offer customized investment management solutions. However, the growing demands of this affluent investor group have evolved.

The account progression is illustrated below.

Brokerage Accounts →Mutual Funds→ Separately Managed Accounts →Unified Managed Accounts

The account options can be generally defined as follows:

Brokerage Accounts – Offer investors the ability to purchase individual securities, but without the professional services of money managers. Brokerage accounts are available with low initial purchase requirements, have minimal asset allocation capacity and require minimal suitability information from the clients to establish.

Mutual Funds – Offer investors professionally managed portfolios, but with limited customization capacity on the individual fund strategies and overall portfolio design. Individual investors are typically charged higher account fees with this option.

Separate accounts, such as the SMA and UMA, offer the ability for an individual investor to gain access to institutional quality portfolio managers in addition to portfolio customization and active tax management.

Separately Managed Accounts – Investment managers are available. A higher minimum opening investment is required to establish these accounts.

Unified Managed Accounts – Offers customized asset allocation models for each individual investor and the ability to implement. Professional investment managers are readily accessible, diversification strategies can be implemented, offer a simple fee structure, require low initial investment requirements (as low as $25,000 per account) and are competitive in terms of annual growth results.

Historically, affluent clients have sought out fee based advisory services, featuring customized investment solutions and recommendations. During the 1970s, the methodology used to develop investment portfolios for the affluent began to change. It was during this era that the use of mutual funds began to emerge. However, investors were at a disadvantage as information asymmetry that was present caused them to seek better investment options and products. Beyond this, capital gains taxes and limited tax flexibility added to the dissatisfaction with mutual funds growing amongst this investor class. SMAs were developed in the 1970s as a solution to address these investor concerns.

Until today, investors seeking professional money managers were limited to Separately Managed Accounts (SMAs). Technology was the enabler of SMAs. SMAs, as favorable as they were initially, are not perfect products. Individual investors began to take note, realizing that their investment returns were negatively impacted by limited investment selections and high fees; hence the development of the UMA.

UMAs of today now offer the ability to capitalize on professional money manager skill sets with less hassle, more transparent fee structures and convenient account monitoring and access capabilities. An UMA offers the ability to accommodate institutional managers, ETFs, mutual funds and bonds within a single account, opened with one application, with one associated fee and available for review on a single account statement.

While these accounts were initially only available to the wealthiest clients due to technology restrictions, the account type is beginning to make sense for most affluent households. In an attempt to provide accessibility to investors, turnkey management providers (TAMPs) have been developed in parallel to UMAs, attempting to build a more cohesive managed account program. TAMPs are the outsourced solution that allows virtually any broker-dealer to compete within the UMA space.

UMAs best serve those investors seeking some degree of tax management which cannot be achieved using mutual funds alone, and who do not have the level of assets to achieve diversification using separately managed accounts.

Chapter 2
The Basics of UMAs

A UMA can be defined as a single account that has the capacity to hold a selection of investment products allocated to an individual client. These investment vehicles enable firms and financial advisors to create efficient investment solutions, using sophisticated portfolio management techniques for their investors.

UMA Functions

The primary functions of an UMA include:

- Cash management
- Tax loss harvesting across investment sleeves
- Rebalancing options, including automatic rebalancing, across managers and asset classes
- Asset allocation based upon the client's risk profile
- Fee calculation on the portfolio as to the associated fees

SMA Benefits

The primary benefits to the client who chooses to place their assets within UMAs include:

- Customization capability of investments

- Open architecture
- Due diligence performed by a variety of investment managers
- Convenience of having a single account
- Ease of manager and asset class comparison
- Automatic investment rebalancing allowing for the avoidance of overweighting in asset classes
- Consolidated tax data, reporting and attribution

Primary UMA Components

The primary components of a UMA include:

Asset Allocation – Asset class categories often respond differently to varying market conditions, displaying different return and risk characteristics. Modern Portfolio Theory suggests that allocating a portfolio across different asset classes chosen to complement an investor's risk tolerance, investment objectives, available capital and investment timeframe can produce the maximum level of return for any chosen level of risk.

Strategic and tactical asset allocation models are diversified across asset classes and styles, ranging from conservative to aggressive risk tolerance levels. These portfolio strategies are available for both taxable and non-taxable investors. Once an asset allocation has been chosen and implemented for a given portfolio, market movements over time will cause portfolio allocations to stray, causing increased exposure to market risk for the individual investor. To combat this risk, UMAs often offer an automatic rebalancing feature, correcting the portfolio by returning it to its original allocation targets on a period basis.

Professional Overlay Management – UMAs offer automatic portfolio rebalancing, enabling investors to maintain their desired asset class and investment style objectives. A UMA's overlay portfolio managers coordinate all activity within the account on behalf of the investor. Overlay refers to the management of individual accounts or sleeves by an individual or technology. Overlay is contrasted with the former SMAs, where investment direction was given to 3rd party managers, removing client managers from the position of investment control.

There are two primary types of vendors within the overlay space – overlay tool providers and overlay managers, Overlay tool providers offer a specific software platform which must be integrated with the managed account platform. Overlay managers deliver investment advisory services and are therefore subject to regulatory and fiduciary responsibilities.

UMA Methodologies

There are a variety of methodologies used in overlay tools and processes.

Passive vs. Active Overlay

Passive overlay involves the separate account managers continuing to perform trading, operational and legal functions for their sleeves. Overlay roles are limited to account allocations and reconciliations. Active overlay management leverages the skill sets of a single overlay manager to assume discretion for a client's accounts. The net result of active overlay management is improved tax optimization, operational efficiency and portfolio customization.

Distributed vs. Centralized Overlay

Distributed overlay refers to the process when a relationship manager established individual rules designed to manage individual client accounts. Centralized overlay decisions are made at the firm level.

Full Service Overlay Professional Managers

A full service OPM will:

1. Actively Trade the Portfolio
2. Coordinate and Improve Tax Strategies
3. Coordinate Account Re-Balancing Requirements
4. Manage Portfolio Risks

The OPM coordinates tax management strategies, such as identifying which lots are for selling and by policy washing sales. The OPM coordinates account rebalancing as the client makes additional contributions or account withdrawals.

In the most basic function, an OPM fulfills an administrative function on behalf of the investor and is a key component of a UMA.

In its most basic terms, overlay is what provides the driving force for UMAs, allowing them to realize their fullest potential.

Range of Investment Products – Investors have access to a range of investment products within an ideal UMA, including:

- Separately Managed Accounts
- ETFs
- Mutual Funds
- Alternative Investments
- Individual Securities
- Bank accounts and CDs
- Fixed income securities
- Commodities, including spot, physical and futures

- Foreign exchange
- Real estate
- Collectibles and art

Because building an UMA that can accommodate and track information on all of these asset classes is important to most investors, most accounts will offer a select list of investment types to their investors, placing some limitations on investment choice.

Tax Management – Many investors focus their attention on their portfolios before tax performance. However, taxes can impact their long term investment strategy, in some cases, outweighing their short term performance results. Therefore, taxes are typically a critical issue facing investors, particularly those in higher federal income tax brackets. UMAs offer the functionality to meet an investor's differing tax needs. For example, some UMAs offer optional tax-loss harvesting and other techniques to manage an investor's taxes at their portfolio level. When these strategies are coupled with processes used by the overlay manager, capital gains can be offset in many cases within the portfolio.

Investment Management – There are four primary approaches to how the UMA's money manager delivers their end results:

1. *Model-Based Delivery* – The discretion for investment management decisions are divided between the investment model and the overlay portfolio managers.
2. *Split Delivery* – The discretion of the investment manager is divided between the overlay portfolio managers and the sponsor firm.
3. *Transitional Delivery* – The investment manager maintains discretion over the investment model and the client's account.

4. *Combination Delivery* – The investment manager utilizes a combination of model deliveries within a single UMA program.

The current model dominating the UMA niche is model-based.

Primary Benefits of UMAs

Investors	Financial Advisors
Improves portfolio diversification	Streamlines account administration, freeing up time to spend on client relationships
Provides comprehensive portfolio management	Strengthens the client-advisor relationship
Focus on consolidated performance rather than product-specific performance	Systematizes client investment solutions and approaches
Delivers a more comprehensive product mix at a more competitive cost	More efficient delivery system of product solutions to the end investor

The delivery of a more comprehensive set of products and services at a competitive price to the end investor will drive the future use of UMA products.

Chapter 3
The Investment Options within UMAs

Individual investors have a variety of investment options to select from within UMAs, including mutual funds, individual securities, ETFs, SMAs and alternative investments.

Mutual Funds

Mutual funds comprise an assortment of individual stocks and bonds. Funds from investors are pooled together, whereby individual investors own a percentage of the pool of funds, represented by their pro-rata share of initial investment. There are several advantages to this form of investment, including:

- Professional Management – Mutual funds are managed by designated portfolio managers, responsible for making investment purchase and sale decisions on behalf of the investor pool.
- Diversification – When individual investors own mutual fund shares; their risk is diluted across multiple underlying securities.
- Economies of Scale – Because mutual funds purchase and sell large quantities of securities, transaction costs to the investor

are lower than what they would pay individually if they ex-
ecuted the same transaction volume.

- Liquidity – Like an individual security, mutual funds offer individual investors the opportunity to request that their shares be
converted to cash at will.

Exchange Traded Funds

ETFs have been rapidly growing in popularity among individual investors over the past decade. In the most basic of terms, ETFs trade
on the stock exchange in a similar fashion as mutual funds. The
performance of an ETF is based upon a chosen underlying index,
which is the basis for how the ETF is replicated. Because ETFs are
designed to track an index, they are considered to be passively managed, unlike mutual funds, which feature active portfolio management. ETFs not only cover the major indexes, but a broader range of
investment options.

There are several reasons why ETFs are growing in popularity
among individual investors, including:

- *Tax Efficiency* – Because of their passive management status,
they tend to offer more favorable tax status than mutual funds
to individual investors.
- *Transparency* – Because ETFs are designed to model their underlying indexes, investors have clarity around what constitutes
the investment. Investors also have easy access to the fees associated with the ETF, adding another dimension of transparency.
- *Reduced Fees* – One of the primary reasons individual investors
are flocking to ETFs is for their relatively low fees, particularly
in comparison to their counterparts – mutual funds.

Alternative Investments

Those products that fall outside the traditional purchase of stocks and bonds are referred to as alternative investments. For example, hedge funds, private equity and real estate are examples of alternative investments available to individual investors both outside and within UMAs. Investors are often attracted to these options due to the potential to offer risk adjusted performance with asset class diversification.

Other investment options available within an UMA can include:

- Bank accounts and CDs
- Fixed income securities
- Commodities, including spot, physical and futures
- Foreign exchange
- Collectibles and art

The capacity to hold alternative investments will be based upon the UMA's architecture and reporting structure.

Chapter 4
Comparing UMAs to SMAs

While there are some fundamental similarities between a UMA and SMA platform, each offers advantages and disadvantages, which both financial advisors and clients should explore when implementing a financial plan.

UMAs

A UMA is a single account designed to enable an investor's asset allocation to be implemented and periodically re-balanced using a combination of investments – ETFs, mutual funds, individual securities, SMAs and alternative investments. UMAs allow investors to combine investments that traditional investment vehicles may not accommodate. Because the asset allocation capabilities are flexible within a UMA, investors can modify their strategies as their goals change over time.

UMAs often offer an active tax management feature. These programs are most commonly offered as fee based, which may be higher in annual cost than a mutual fund wrap program. UMA fees tend to be greater when investment allocations favor equities and decline as asset levels rise.

UMA Features

- Professional money management
- Asset allocation capacity
- Product neutral
- Flexibility
- Active tax management
- Overlay managers assigned to each account
- Single 1099s issued to investors
- Single account statement
- Periodic account rebalancing
- Multiple investment managers

One of the primary benefits of UMAs is that they are a 'just right' solution when mutual funds are too limited and SMAs are too large.

SMAs

Separately managed accounts offer asset allocation focused investment choices, but require investors to open several accounts to achieve equivalent diversification to a UMA. This diversification is coupled with the added consequence of 1099s issued to the investor for each of the separate accounts. Because separate accounts are required for each asset class, this investment strategy requires a higher initial investment amount than a UMA.

SMA Programs versus UMA Programs

While there are a variety of distinct differences between both investment platforms, there are key distinct differences worth noting.

1. *Fewer Sponsor-Manager Linkages* – Fewer communication linkages are required in a UMA world as the overlay portfolio manager acts as a hub, consolidating communication transactions.

2. *Fewer Accounts* – Because UMAs leverage a consolidated account, fewer accounts are required for the end investor to achieve the same level of diversification. Within a SMA environment, an investor may be required to have several asset strategies, each requiring its own separate brokerage account. UMAs combine these separate brokerage accounts into a single custodial account.

3. *More Data Per Account* – Despite the reduction in total accounts within a UMA environment, each independent UMA carries additional data elements. Individual UMAs carry associated information, such as holdings, investment vehicles and asset allocation information. Because lower investment minimums are permitted, it is common for investors to have 4–5 strategies, whereas in the past, they would have had 2–3 strategies using SMA.

4. *Emerging Information* – Communication between the investment manager and the overlay portfolio manager represents an emerging communications infrastructure.

5. *Cost Effectiveness*- UMAs are more cost effective than SMAs. Instead of the client paying 80–100bp for an SMA sleeve, their cost is often reduced to 30–40bp when leveraging UMAs due to the overlay tool.

Chapter 5
How Financial Advisors Utilize UMAs to Attract Affluent Clients

The environment facing financial advisors today is complex, competitive and ever-changing. In order to succeed, financial advisors must learn to adapt to the changing landscape, adopting best practices utilized by industry leaders.

In January 2005, CEG Worldwide conducted a comprehensive survey of 1,028 independent broker-dealers. While the definition of success varies from person to person, income is utilized in this study to delineate success levels of those surveyed.

The results of this survey suggest that 50% of wealth managers working with Turnkey Asset Management Providers (TAMPs), earned between $500,000–749,000 in 2004. None of the advisors within this group earned less than $100,000. Non-TAMP investment generalists earned the least amount of income.

Overall, a wealth management business model and an affiliate with a TAMP contributed to the greatest level of financial success.

UMAs offer the greatest benefit for the top two client segments – high net worth households ($2 million to $10 million) and ultra-high net worth households ($10 million+). Previously, wealth investors were treated as institutional investors, faced with the requirement to meet the minimum amounts that large institutional customers were required to satisfy.

What types of products are these top financial advisors offering to their clients?

The CEG Worldwide study revealed fundamental differences between investment generalists and wealth managers. Investments were a relatively insignificant offering for wealth managers. Only 56.7% of the wealth manager group offered a fee based investment to a top 20 client, while nearly 75% of the investment generalists surveyed offered a fee based product to their top clients. This result suggests that wealth managers are more successful in delivering more comprehensive financial solutions to their top clients.

Wealth managers provided estate planning, life insurance, income tax planning, charitable giving planning, and asset allocation planning services to their clients during the 6 months prior to completing this survey. Virtually none of the investment generalists focused on these services with their clients.

How do Top Advisors Find Affluent Clients?

One of the primary focus areas for financial advisors, regardless of success level, is sourcing wealthy clients. The CEG study found that top financial advisors sourced their top clients from referrals, particularly from another professional such as a CPA or attorney. Other lead sources for top advisors include referrals from existing top clients and topic focused seminars.

The Move to Wealth Management – Integrating UMAs

1. **Lead with a Profit Center** – Investment planning is often the most profitable service for most financial advisors. Therefore, advisors should lead with it moving forward. From here, advisors can begin to address a client's additional financial needs – protection planning, estate planning, and comprehensive financial planning.

2. **Form Strategic Alliances** – Most financial advisors lack the infrastructure or expertise to offer a full spectrum of wealth management products and services to their clients independently. Therefore, wealth managers form strategic alliances with other professionals for access to the expertise that their clients demand. These alliances enable financial advisors to expand their wealth management offerings, giving them the ability to deliver truly comprehensive solutions to their clients. This ability commands the greatest value within the marketplace. A best practice is to explore strategic alliances with attorneys who serve high net worth clients, with complex financial needs, as wealth management strategies are adept at solving.

3. **Charge Asset Based Fees** – Shift from transactional based relationships to an asset based fee model when working in the investment planning niche. It is important to note that your practice need not be 100% fee based, as the top wealth managers leverage a variety of products and services to meet the needs of their clients.

4. **Leverage Wealth Management Tools** – Many financial advisors experience practice management challenges as their practices expand. How do you balance client service meetings, marketing and lead generation activities, developing client solutions and keeping up with investment research simultaneously? While it may be straightforward to manage these tasks

initially, as a practice grows, a financial advisor's time begins to stretch. Many professionals ultimately arrive at the conclusion that they are better suited acting in the role of a financial consultant rather than as a money manager. Financial consultants provide advice and direction for a variety of areas, including estate planning, protection planning and tax planning, tapping into the skill sets and resources of niche specific professionals as needed rather than attempting to be all things to all people. Those advisors who implement this concept effectively often experience phenomenal practice growth and success.

Chapter 6
The UMA Competitive Landscape

UMAs act as a key resource for advisors seeking to provide wealth management services to their affluent clients. This investment vehicle is influencing business models across the financial services industry, significantly impacting how advisors deliver investment solutions to their clients. UMA concepts and options will continue to evolve.

Top UMAs offer solutions that encompass asset allocation, mutual funds and portfolio manager selection, SMAs, performance reports, back office support and marketing tools for advisors. Wealth managers who utilize UMAs are essentially outsourcing these responsibilities, freeing up their time to focus on their most important role – client relationships.

Virtually every major financial institution has either developed or considered developing UMA, or UMA like solutions. When choosing UMAs to partner with, advisors should evaluate four primary areas:

1. **UMA Value** – How does the UMA differ from other available solutions? How does the UMA deliver value to the client?

2. **Service Value** – How does the UMA provide support value for the advisor? i.e. marketing support, practice management concepts, regulatory management and training programs, reporting capabilities and technology support.
3. **Personal Value** – What daily value is delivered by the UMA in terms of operations and business development?
4. **Image Value** – How does the UMA's image resonate with clients and prospects? i.e. brand power

Size of the UMA Market

According to the Money Management Institute, the current UMA market is estimated to be near $40 billion. However, this may be a low estimate, as it does not include 'rep as portfolio manager' sleeves. Total managed solutions are growing relative to the markets, in particular, as much as 54% over the past 2 years.

The top ten programs by size, based upon data from the 2007 Money Management Institute report, currently include:

1. Smith Barney (Citigroup)
2. Merrill Lynch
3. Wachovia
4. Morgan Stanley
5. UBS
6. Charles Schwab
7. Bank of America
8. Lockwood Financial
9. SunGard Advisor
10. Raymond James

TAMP Sponsors

Envestnet

The Envestnet UMA web-based platform is fully integrated, allowing financial advisors the opportunity to successfully manage their client's accounts using their all-in-one functionality. The tasks of client servicing are automated, allowing advisors to focus more of their time and attention on building and shaping their practice. The Envestnet platform can be implemented on a stand-alone or fully-integrated basis. Their platform also makes it simple to merge existing proprietary products and custodial relationships. Within their UMA structure, advisors have access to over 80 leading institutional managers, with reduced minimum initial investments.

Fundquest

The Fundquest UMA offers financial advisors the following features:

- The ability to customize a client's accounts by restricting specific securities
- Proactive tax management strategies
- On-demand proposal technology with integrated profiling, research and portfolio diagnostics
- Quarterly and online performance reporting capabilities
- Sales support
- Advanced back office administration

Their overlay management system coordinates the UMA portfolio across the underlying investment products. Their overall overlay management process is to coordinate buy/sell/hold opportunities, to implement client-specific customization, to rebalance to targeted allocations and to process tax harvesting requests. This overall process results in coordination of investment managers and styles across product selections, to diversify the overall portfolio and to provide an integrated portfolio view for both the advisor and the client.

The minimum account balance with Fundquest is $250,000.

Geneworth

Geneworth currently offers three primary portfolio strategies within their UMA platform; Active Return Opportunities (ARO), Genworth Multiple Strategy Portfolios (GMS) and Privately Managed Portfolios (PMP). The UMA focused investment management firms within these three primary UMA strategies include: Evercore Asset Management, Epoch Investment Partners, Inc., Deerborn Partners Inc., Lotsoft Capital Management LLC, Delaware Investments Inc., Marvin & Palmer Assoc. Inc., Clay Finlay Inc., Voyager Asset Management and Levin Capital Strategies, LP. Their UMA structure houses stocks, fixed income products, mutual funds, ETFs and alternative investments under a single umbrella. The current minimum investment for the Genworth UMAs is $50,000.

Brinker Capital

The Brinker Capital UMA programs offers the ability to develop highly customized portfolio strategies for clients using over 70 institutional managers and separate account strategies.

Bellatore, LLC/Legion Portfolio

The primary benefit of working with Bellatore is their back end support structure. In addition to the regular reporting performed by the individual advisor, Bellatore works to re-adjust the client's portfolio back to its original asset allocation on a periodic basis. This process ensures that the client remains in their ideal portfolio allocation.

Their reporting process allows for both the advisor and the client to review their progress at the portfolio level and asset class levels. Statements are sent quarterly, providing an easy to read break down of all pertinent account information. Annually, the client and the advisor will receive tax statements, trade confirmations and overall account statements.

Overlay Management and Technology

Technology providers are categorized based upon their scope and product offerings. Each UMA utilizes broad technology platforms that generally have accounting functions at their core. Their primary purpose is to act as an end-to-end solution for managers and sponsors.

Below is a list of the top overlay management/technology service providers.

Parametric – Parametric provides a structured portfolio management solution. Parametric's overlay management program offers coordination and implementation of the client account. Their overlay manager role encompasses rebalancing, trading, cash flows and tax management. One of the primary features of this system includes the ability to manage tax liability. Some of the features of this system include:

- Avoidance of wash sale violations
- Short term gain deferral
- Daily active tax loss harvesting
- Transition of pre-existing securities to minimize turnover in a tax aware fashion

The Overlay platform offers several rebalancing options based upon percentages, sponsor-directed rules or a combination.

Adhesion – Originally focused on large financial institutions, this platform is now available to the RIA market. Adhesion's WealthADV platforms works both as an end-to-end solution and as a separate module. WealthADV offers a variety of key features when performing in an overlay portfolio manager role:

- Ongoing account monitoring
- Automatic account rebalancing
- The ability to implement manager model changes
- Client billing of fees

Performance is calculated using a proprietary engine, which allows for rapid daily time weighted returns, which consider all cash flows. All reports are offered both at the household and sleeve level.

Tamarac – Tamarac is web-based software for investment professionals. Its overlay tool is a web-based rebalancing and trade order generation system that works with an unlimited account capacity. Some of the other key features of this platform include:

- Restriction capabilities – legacy positions can be eliminated or restricted during account rebalancing, there are multiple ways to oversee accounts and security or industry group restrictions are supported at the individual and family account levels
- Cash management – Cash can be raised or invested simultaneously across multiple accounts and custom cash settings can be utilized
- Fee Tracking
- Tax Loss Harvesting – Automatic capacity to identify tax lots which can be sold in a tax efficient manner
- Rebalancing Engine
- Flexible Integration – Portfolio management reporting and back office support

Smartleaf – This overlay tool is used primarily by bank trust companies and other fiduciaries. This highly automated tool allows trust companies to offer fully integrated solutions for the benefit of their investment management clients. Because of this overlay solution, financial institutions have the capacity to manage individual accounts on a customized basis. One of the primary differences between Smartleaf and other providers is that they do not act as asset managers themselves. Because of this difference, this platform is more attractive to trust companies and RIAs where the advisor has already accepted fiduciary responsibilities. The Smartleaf solution does not provide manager due diligence, but like most overlay tools, enables investment organizations to manage other components – risk, trading expenses, account restrictions and taxes.

The Smartleaf tool provides an open architecture while also offering:

- Improved cost over SMAs
- The ability for culture matching, where security selection can be outsourced without also outsourcing fiduciary responsibilities
- All transactions are completed through the overlay tool allowing for custodial arrangements to be managed in a single location
- The ability to customize portfolios

Smartleaf can be used in either a centralized or distributed environment.

Vestmark – Provides privately branded technology serving the underlying systems for UMA sponsored firms. This system enables open architecture while providing appropriate linkability between all players within the managed account space. This is a technology platform, therefore it does not offer due diligence capacity for individual managers. It does however provide a working framework for administering approved managers.

Vestmark models include:

- Account opening and administration
- Order and execution management
- Overlay management
- Portfolio accounting and reporting
- Asset allocation and portfolio design
- Compliance and audit trails
- Model management

The Vestmark platform can handle SMA sleeves, active and passive sleeves, as well as mutual funds, ETFs, fixed income securities and alternative investments. The PORTIA accounting system offered by Thomson is utilized by Vestmark. One of the most attractive features to advisors is that the system is highly scalable and browser-based.

Custodians Connected with TAMP Platforms
Schwab
TD Institutional
Fidelity
Trust Company of America

Chapter 7
The Future of Managed Money and Unified Managed Accounts

Many advisors and industry leaders believe that investment management will continue to be commoditized over the next 5 years. According to the CEG study referenced earlier, nearly all wealth managers (91.9%) predict that the leading business model for the future will focus on providing multiple products and services to clients, including UMAs. UMAs are currently the fastest growing segment within the managed account industry.

While SMAs hold a significant portion of the movable assets, investors are modifying their investment strategy as they are seeking to diversify their investments, finding limitations within their current account structure (SMA). Therefore, industry leaders as well as individual investors look to the UMA as representing the future of the industry. Model based portfolio programs are expected to see the largest growth within the UMA market.

Acceptance that affluent clients will continue to be a driving force for industry success is prevalent among top advisors. For advisors looking to maximize their financial success, there are several key strategies worth consideration and adoption, including transferring to a practice based upon wealth management philosophies.

Transition to Wealth Management

Advisors will find themselves faced with a variety of practice management decisions throughout their careers. Should they outsource money management responsibilities? Should they work on a fee based or commission structure? While choosing solutions can present challenges to advisors, when they choose the right professional partners, their business will not only grow, but they will often feel re-energized. Both of these outcomes will lead to positive business change.

The concept of wealth management focuses on building long term, consultative relationships with clients. This involves providing a wide array of product offerings to clients, such as estate planning, asset protection and integrated investment solutions. Based upon the research referenced earlier by CEG, a wealth management business model is superior to one that is investment focused. The consultative nature of a wealth management strategy allows wealth managers to focus on the needs of the affluent market by offering a broad range of complex solutions, while simultaneously enhancing client relationships.

If these conclusions are true, why don't more financial advisors adopt these strategies?

Bibliography

1. Robert J. Ellis, and Uzair Nasim, Unified Managed Accounts, Development in UMAs and Overlay Technology to Provide Total Client Solutions, January 2009, Celent.
2. The Asset Management Industry in 2010, McKinsey&Company, 2009.
3. Unified Managed Account, FundQuest, A BNP Paribas Company,2009.
4. Envestnet OS Brochure Chart, 2009.
5. Sonaimuthu, N, Vicki Morris, 2007 Wealth Management Best Practices: A Practical Guide, White Paper by Infosys Technologies Limited, 2007.
6. The Future of Advice, Financial Institutions Research Report, Tiburon Strategic Advisors, 2005.
7. The Evolution from a Platform Provider to Investment Management Firm, Brinker Capital, 2009.
8. Adviser Services Map, Investnet, 2009.
9. Unified Managed Accounts: Bringing Institutional Investing to Individual Investor, Brinker Capital, 2009.
10. Unified Managed Accounts and Model Portfolios: Poised for Growth, But Can the Industry Support it? A report prepared by the Depository Trust & Clearing Corporation, 2008.

Biography

Since 2000, Jason Lampa has been helping financial professionals reach new levels of achievement by facilitating new ways of thinking and innovative marketing programs. Having worked withthousands of independent financial professionals both in the US and abroad, Jason brings a unique perspective and an abundance of new ideas to the financial services community. There are two main benefits that Jason brings to those professionals with whom he partners:

1. The ability to segment demographics and come up with unique strategies that the financial services industry hasn't embraced yet (e.g. social media strategies for financial advisors).
2. The responsibility he feels he owes to his clients to keep abreast of domestic and international financial markets. Jason is well-versed in multiple product lines within the financial services industry, including: separately managed accounts, unified managed accounts, hedge funds, pension plans, options, private placements and real estate.

"I believe that financial advisors understand the need to differentiate their business from their competition through a distinct, repeatable process that brings results." As part of his effort to provide high impact solutions for financial professionals, Jason writes a monthly column for ProducersWeb – a leading online media publication. He was recently added as the expert for baby boomer marketing trends. "My relationship with my clients is 95/5. I will put in 95% of the effort, you put in 5 %. You may find it hard to think of relationships in your life that provide you the same benefit."